The Decentralized World

Understanding Blockchain's Potential Impact on Global Economy

Table of Contents

Chapter 1. Introduction

Navigating through the synchronized cadence of technology and economy, we've designed this Special Report titled "The Decentralized World: Understanding Blockchain's Potential Impact on Global Economy," specifically for those curious about the evolving digital landscapes. This report doesn't demand a technical background, instead, it takes the reader by the hand – elucidating complex terminologies with riveting analogies, subsequently unveiling the transformative potential of blockchain on our economy. Through this voyage, the reader will discover how elegantly this technology intertwines with everyday life, offering a fresh perspective on financial systems, governance, and global trade. Don't shy away from the future, embrace it, and let this eye-opening report be your compass as it navigates the innovative, promising, yet frequently mystifying world of decentralized systems.

Chapter 2. Demystifying Blockchain: A Thorough Introduction

In the bustling world of digital innovation, one term continues to reverberate across Silicon Valley, investment forums, and economic roundtables worldwide - "blockchain". In simplest words, a blockchain is like a decentralized digital ledger. But what does that mean? To understand this, let's embark on an enlightening sojourn.

2.1. Understanding Blockchain Basics

Suppose you're playing a game of poker with friends, but there is no dealer. How do you ensure no one is cheating? You could record each transaction (bet, call, or raise) publically. Everyone could have a copy of this public record and each time a transaction is made, it's recorded by everyone. This is the basic idea of blockchain - a public ledger detailing 'transactions', managed by a network of computers that are all updating and agreeing on the contents of this ledger.

If we go back to our poker analogy, each round could be seen as a 'block' of transactions; once completed, it's added to a 'chain' of previous rounds or blocks. Only when everyone in the game agrees on the validity of the transactions in a block, it can be added to the chain.

Blockchain is thus a type of distributed ledger technology (DLT), where the ledger is maintained and updated by multiple nodes (computers) in the network.

2.2. The Underlying Tenets of Blockchain

The appeal of using blockchain is in its key features: Decentralization, Transparency, and Immutability.

Decentralization: Unlike traditional databases that are governed by a centralized authority, blockchain distributes its ledger across numerous nodes. This means there is no single point of failure, and no central authority can tamper with the data.

Transparency: While user identities are secured through complex cryptography, the actions of an individual user (their transactions) are visible to all members of the network. This promotes accountability and trust within the system.

Immutability: Once a block is added to the chain, it's near to impossible to change that block's data. This immutable nature of blockchain assures the integrity and authenticity of all transactions.

2.3. Blockchain's Under-the-Hood: Blocks and Chains

Each 'block' in a blockchain contains a list of transactions. Along with that, two notable elements are 'Hash' and 'Previous Block Hash'.

A Hash is a unique code, similar to a fingerprint for humans. Changes in the transaction data within a block will lead to a change in this Hash. The Previous Block Hash element links a block to the block before it, forming a chain. As a result, if a hacker tries to alter the data inside a block, its Hash will change, causing the chain to break.

To resume a normal chain, the hacker will have to change the Hash in each subsequent block, which is computationally impossible due to the Proof of Work system implemented in blockchain technology. This makes blockchain incredibly secure and resistant to fraudulent activity.

2.4. Common Types of Blockchain

There are three main types of blockchain with unique characteristics: Public, Private, and Consortium blockchain.

Public blockchain is completely open-source, allowing anyone to participate as a user, miner, or developer. It's fully decentralized with no one in complete control. Bitcoin and Ethereum are good examples.

On the other hand, Private blockchains are used within a single organization. Here, the organization has complete control over who can read the blockchain, submit transactions, and validate them.

A Consortium blockchain is a semi-decentralized type. Here, a select group of nodes is given the authority to approve transactions, making it a hybrid between a public and private blockchain.

2.5. The Confluence of Blockchain and Economy

Blockchain technology holds the potential to revolutionize numerous facets of the global economy by providing a secure, transparent, and decentralized method to record transactions. Financial services, supply chain management, intellectual property rights, and voting systems are a few sectors that can greatly benefit from the utilization of blockchain tech.

The road to a decentralized world might pose challenges up front. But the potential benefits make this journey compelling. Embrace blockchain with open arms, explore the opportunities it presents, and leverage it as an enlightening compass navigating the expansive digital frontiers. Together, we shall forge our path ahead in this Decentralized World.

Chapter 3. The Fundamentals: Understanding the Science Behind Blockchain

With the advent of Bitcoin in 2009, the technology world was exposed to one of the most critical technologies in modern times: blockchain. This technology, considered the backbone of cryptocurrencies such as Bitcoin and Ethereum, has the potential to transform various sectors from finance to governance, global trade, supply chain management, health care, and more. To yield the most substantial benefits from blockchain and understand its economic implications, it is crucial to fathom its fundamental workings.

3.1. Unraveling The Concept: What Is Blockchain?

The term "blockchain" can be broken down into two words – 'block' and 'chain.' It's akin to a digital ledger comprising a 'chain' of 'blocks,' with every 'block' storing an identical copy of the digital transaction data from a single, or a series of transactions. Much like a spreadsheet that is spread across various computers in a decentralized network, each transaction gets registered in a 'block,' and every block is chained to its former, thus forming a blockchain.

This decentralized, distributive ledger recording transactions across multiple computers ensures that any involved record cannot be altered retroactively, prohibiting the modification of subsequent blocks - thus, rendering the system secure. Here, the security emanates from the decentralization; not being controlled by a single entity and its existence on multiple systems makes it hard to manipulate or hack.

3.2. The integral elements of Blockchain: Understanding Its Key Components

At its essence, a blockchain system consists of three main components – a network of computers (nodes), the ledger, and the consensus algorithm.

3.2.1. Nodes

Each computer within the blockchain network is referred to as a node. When a transaction occurs, it's the nodes that are responsible for validating them. Each node retains an identical copy of the blockchain, ensuring the security and integrity of the data.

3.2.2. Ledger

The ledger can be seen as an exhaustive record book that keeps track of every transaction since the inception of the blockchain, available for public viewing. Stored across the network on each node, it maintains transparency, eradicates the need for intermediaries, and ensures absolute data integrity.

3.2.3. Consensus Algorithm

The consensus algorithm is a protocol underpinning the blockchain, which nodes use to agree on a single version of the blockchain. Two of the most frequently used consensus algorithms are Proof-of-Work (PoW) and Proof-of-Stake (PoS).

3.3. Decoding The Mechanics: How Does Blockchain Work?

Every transaction in the blockchain undergoes a series of steps before becoming part of the immutable ledger.

3.3.1. Transaction Is Made

The process initiates when a transaction is made, where the transaction details are bundled with others into a block.

3.3.2. Block Verification

Nodes spread across the network then receive this block. They validate the transactions within the block, ensuring they are true and not fraudulent.

3.3.3. Consensus

Once verified, nodes reach a specific consensus method established in the protocol, such as mining in a PoW system or voting in a PoS system. This consensus phase provides cryptographic proof that the transactions are valid.

3.3.4. Block Addition

Upon reaching consensus, the new block, containing a unique cryptographic signature (or hash), is added to the existing chain of blocks. This addition is then reflected across the entire network – updating every copy of the ledger almost simultaneously.

3.4. Reflection Upon Security: Blockchain's Immutability and Transparency

The cryptographic hashing and consensus protocols intrinsic to blockchain render the system secure and almost impenetrable. Once a block becomes part of the chain, altering the associated data becomes computationally impractical, reinforcing the immutability of blockchain. Each block contains the hash of itself and the previous block, stitching them together. Therefore, to alter a block would require changing all subsequent blocks, an effort too laborious and conspicuous given the consensus requirement.

Moreover, the distributed ledger system ensures absolute transparency, where all transactions are visible to anyone within the network. Despite being visible, the cryptographic nature of these transactions provides an essential layer of privacy and protection for the user identities.

3.5. The Future: The Usages Of Blockchain Beyond Cryptocurrency

While blockchain is often synonymous with cryptocurrency, especially Bitcoin, its real potential lies much beyond. Blockchain technology has the potential to disrupt numerous sectors for its core attributes of decentralization, transparency, and security.

3.5.1. Blockchain in Financial Services:

Blockchain can fundamentally transform financial services, removing intermediaries in transactions, lowering costs and increasing speed and efficiency. Smart Contracts, an algorithm within a blockchain, can execute financial transactions once predefined conditions are met, streamlining complex processes.

3.5.2. Blockchain in Supply Chain:

In supply chain management, blockchain provides real-time, end-to-end transparency of goods, helping to counteract counterfeiting, reduce losses, and increase consumer trust.

3.5.3. Blockchain in Healthcare:

In healthcare, patient records can be securely encrypted and shared across multiple providers, ensuring data privacy and improving care coordination.

Unraveling the world of blockchain technology reveals a complex, yet elegantly designed system with immense potential to reshape the globe, disrupting the traditional norms of transaction and data management. As we continue to explore this decentralized world, it seems inevitable that blockchain will form an integral part of our digital future.

Chapter 4. Blockchain and Cryptocurrency: A Deep Connection

The journey to understanding the deep connection between blockchain technology and cryptocurrency begins with an exploration into their origin and purpose. As we delve into this intriguing subject, we'll expound on the principles that drive these innovations and illustrate how they've become so inextricable.

4.1. Origin Story: Blockchain and Cryptocurrency

Their conjoined birth happened in 2008 when an individual or group known by the pseudonym Satoshi Nakamoto published a whitepaper detailing a novel electronic cash system, Bitcoin - a new form of digital currency, or cryptocurrency. What made this system unique, groundbreaking even, was the foundational technology that powered it – the blockchain.

By design, cryptocurrencies employ blockchain as an underlying framework. Blockchain provides a transparent and immutable ledger that records transactions across many computers - with no need for a central point of authority, such as a bank or governmental institution. This subsequently fosters trustless, peer-to-peer transactions.

4.2. Unique Identities, Joined At The Hip

Let's liken blockchain to the skeletal framework of a human body, granting it structure. Similarly, cryptocurrency is likened to the blood coursing through the veins, bringing life to the body. While they possess distinct roles and functionalities, these cannot be separated while keeping their essence preserved.

On the blockchain, each digital currency or token represents an asset, or a value-holder. For example, the Bitcoin blockchain underpins its eponymous cryptocurrency, Bitcoin. Pretty much like the relationship between a vehicle and a road - the road (blockchain) facilitating a framework while the vehicle (cryptocurrency) completes transactions.

4.3. Intertwining Complexities: Blockchain's Chain of Blocks

The blockchain's strength primarily lies in its append-only structure and decentralization. It is essentially a distributed and decentralized ledger of all transactions across a peer-to-peer network. Made up of a sequence of 'blocks,' each block contains a list of transactions and is chained to the preceding block through a cryptographic hash function.

The immutable characteristics of the blockchain enable the efficient verification of transactions. Each new block of transactions contains references to the previous block of transactions, making alterations almost impossible without disrupting the entire chain.

4.4. Cryptocurrency: More Than Mere Money

While often likened to digital money, cryptocurrencies serve purposes far beyond this simplistic analogy. As the primary application of blockchain technology, these digital tokens enable asset ownership representation, facilitate smart contracts, and enact as a medium of exchange. Though cryptocurrency's potential is limitless, its current ecosystem is not without its caveats - price volatility, regulatory challenges, and adoption issues.

4.5. Shared Principles: Decentralization and Trustlessness

The symbiotic pairing of blockchain and cryptocurrency emerges from their shared principles of decentralization and trustlessness. Decentralization ensures the system doesn't favor any particular user or party and removes central points of failure. Trustlessness allows participants to interact with each other without needing to trust a central authority or intermediary.

Users can make transactions with cryptocurrencies on a blockchain network, confident of their validity and permanence. There's a guarantee of accuracy, as the system is constantly in agreement - an attribute known as consensus.

4.6. Beyond Currency: Blockchain Expands Its Horizon

Though cryptocurrency remains blockchain's most famed use-case, the latter's potential extends far beyond digital currencies. As its fundamental property implies, blockchain can maintain and validate any type of digital exchange. Be it ownership documents, medical records, votes, or identity verification, blockchain can manage it in a transparent and immutable way.

4.7. Complexity Explored: Cryptographic Security

A key aspect of the blockchain and cryptocurrency relationship is cryptographic security. The term cryptography refers to a method of protecting information through the use of codes so that only the intended person can read and process it. Both blockchain and cryptocurrency involve cryptographic algorithms to ensure data security through the entire transaction process.

4.8. Together Towards Tomorrow: The Road Ahead

Blockchain and cryptocurrency continue to develop together, shaping the future of digital economy. Blockchain's potential applications – from banking to healthcare, from supply chains to legal contracts – mirror the myriad uses of cryptocurrency. As they evolve together, complex issues of scalability, interoperability, and regulation will be central to their growth and influence.

By navigating the interconnected voyage of blockchain and cryptocurrency, we've begun to unravel the complexities of these two dynamic juggernauts. Remember, blockchain and cryptocurrency are more than mere technologies. They represent a paradigm shift in how we perceive trust, security, and decentralization. As their untapped potential becomes explored, we will undoubtedly witness a transformative impact on the global economy.

Chapter 5. Economic Disruption: Blockchain's Potential in Financial Sector

The globe is witnessing an alteration in the zeitgeist across several sectors and industries. One of the prominent sectors, the financial sector, stands precariously on the precipice of this change. The catalyst, you ask? The blockchain, a marvel of digital technology, is the veritable game changer that is overturning traditional models and conversations around what it means to participate in global economics.

5.1. The Primer: Unraveling Blockchain

If one had to draw an analogy, consider blockchain as a digital ledger – akin to a communal spreadsheet maintained in an open, decentralized network. Every transaction is a 'block,' which is recorded, validated, and then appended to the 'chain' of previous transactions. Crucially, these data blocks are interlinked and traceable, which ensures transparency and security while minimizing fraud.

One might wonder why an inherently technical system like the blockchain is causing seismic shifts in an age-old industry. The answer lays in blockchain's inherent properties: its decentralized nature, transparency, accessibility, and security.

5.2. Cascading Changes: Effects on Financial Systems

Coupling these attributes with the financial sector spawns a new breed of financial systems, where power is decentralizing and transparency is paramount. For instance, the current banking systems, controlled by centralized entities, deal with numerous intermediaries, which inflate costs and time scales.

Blockchain, with its peer-to-peer transaction model, bypasses intermediaries, thereby reducing cost and time. Imagine "money" being sent like an email, without the need of any third-party approval or excessive transaction fees. Sounds similar to digital money transfer apps, but it's more secure and unregulated by single entities.

5.3. Bursting The Bubble: Critiques and Counter-Arguments

Despite the promise, blockchain's traverse through the financial sector isn't without its quandaries. They revolve chiefly around the nascent status of the technology, the perceived threat to existing financial power structures, and concerns around customer protection and data privacy.

While the technology is hailed for its security, its decentralization also makes it harder to target and prevent fraudulent activity. Also, its use in facilitating anonymous transactions raises red flags, ushering in skepticism around its adoption.

5.4. Morphing Markets: Cryptocurrencies and ICOs

Blockchain brought along a new form of financial assets, cryptocurrencies, the most famous of which is Bitcoin. These digital currencies are decentralized, secure, and free from governmental regulation. They've found use in a wide variety of sectors, from remittances to investments, but it's their use in Initial Coin Offerings (ICOs) that have really taken the world by storm.

ICOs are a disruptive take on the traditional fundraising model, allowing startups to raise funds directly from investors in exchange for tokens. However, with success stories also come instances of significant financial losses, inviting global regulatory scrutiny.

5.5. Gazing into the Future: Towards Decentralized Finance

As we look ahead, the fusion of the financial sector and blockchain posits the emergence of Decentralized Finance, or DeFi. In this new model, financial services like lending, borrowing, and trading can be navigated via decentralized platforms without the reliance on intermediaries like banks or insurance firms.

By embracing blockchain, we stand on the fringes of a transformative era where control over finances won't be dominated by a few centralized authorities. Instead, it will rest in the hands of those who should genuinely have it: individuals and businesses.

The adoption of blockchain in the financial sector is not a matter of "if" but "when." The road may be paved with obstacles, but as with any major innovation, the path will only get clearer as we make strides towards it.

To sum it up, blockchain persists as a beacon, signalling a brave new world of financial transactions. It's an incipient journey, but one that could very well redefine our notion of a global economy.

Despite its many challenges, the potential it holds for the evolution of finance is tremendous. And so, from public ledgers to cryptocurrencies, ICOs to DeFi, our financial future promises suspense and excitement, as we linger on the cusp of a fascinating era fueled by blockchain. A world beckons where economies aren't just connected, they are decentralized, democratized and above all, resistant to external manipulation. The script is still being written, and the promise of blockchain in redefining our world is simply too intriguing to ignore.

Chapter 6. Decentralized Autonomous Organizations: A New Age Governance

The seismic shift in technology over the past decade has paved the way for harnessing the power of decentralized systems. No longer are decisions and power concentrated with a governing body or a centralized authority. Instead, power is dispersed and shared among the individuals that constitute a system. Central to this idea is the concept of Decentralized Autonomous Organizations (DAOs).

6.1. The Conception and Philosophy of DAOs

In essence, Decentralized Autonomous Organizations or DAOs depict a paradigm shift in how we perceive governance. They promise a fresh approach, with their defining feature being that they run through rules encoded as computer programs known as smart contracts. DAOs live on the blockchain, a decentralized and distributed digital ledger known for its transparency, security, and immutability.

The philosophy of DAOs can be traced back to the innate human desire for freedom, fairness, and autonomy. It aligns with the ethos of peer-to-peer interaction, where the absence of a central authority allows for surplus value created by a network to be distributed amongst its participants in a fair manner.

6.2. Understanding the Mechanics of DAOs

At the heart of every DAO are smart contracts - these are self-executing contracts with the terms of the agreement directly written into lines of code. These programs automatically implement actions based on predefined rules and guidelines. For instance, if X event takes place, then the contract will construe it as an instruction to execute Y action, thereby mitigating any need for manual interference.

DAOs generally operate with a native token - a type of cryptocurrency that participants can own. The tokenization model produces a dual-pronged outcome. Firstly, it provides a medium for members to engage in transactions. Secondly, it gives the owners voting rights, which are proportionate to the number of tokens they own within the system. The process is strikingly democratic, echoing the principles of one person, one vote in its mechanism.

6.3. DAOs: Assembling Communities with Shared Vision

DAOs are a testament to the power of collective community decision making. Participants leveraging their voting rights allows for resources to be allocated in a way which reflects the priorities and values of the community that constitute an organization. This shared sense of purpose and ambition for progress makes DAOs an exciting model for innovation and advancement.

6.4. DAOs in Practice: Examples and Applications

DAOs have found practical applications across various domains. Among the pioneer implementations is "The DAO," an investor-directed venture capital fund built on the Ethereum blockchain. Despite an unfortunate hacking incident that saw it shuttered, it propelled the concept of DAOs into the mainstream.

Another practical instance is "Moloch DAO," focusing on funding Ethereum projects. Distinctly, its design presented "rage quitting" as an innovative solution to the problem of minority exploitation, permitting members to withdraw their shares when they disagree with the majority decision.

"Gnosis' dxDAO" is an additional example, evolved to govern a decentralized trading protocol. It went on to demonstrate that even without a thematic unity or a focused goal, a DAO could still perform efficiently.

6.5. Challenges and Risks

While DAOs present exciting opportunities, they aren't without challenges. For one, there's an inherent risk of code vulnerability due to the complexity and rigidity of smart contracts. The DAO incident is a significant reference point for the same.

Next, legal recognition presents an arduous hurdle. Because DAOs exist outside the realm of traditional regulatory frameworks, they inhabit a world of legal ambiguity.

Personal privacy is another challenge. While the inherent transparency of DAOs has its advantages, it might lead to privacy concerns as interactions are stored publicly on a blockchain.

Moreover, while the concept of DAOs is based on decentralization, the risk of wealth concentration still remains. This poses the question of truly equitable governance.

6.6. The Future of DAOs and Closing Remarks

Despite the challenges, DAOs hold a robust potential to reinvent traditional models of governance. System resilience, democratic decision-making, and disintermediation of authority are just a few of the strengths DAOs can offer. By embedding economic incentives and governance protocols into a transparent and secure digital framework, DAOs might lead governance into a truly automated, decentralized era.

In conclusion, DAOs are challenging our perception of organizational governance. Their emergence posits an intriguing dichotomy of excitement and caution. The journey towards embracing DAOs in our global infrastructure paints an enigmatic yet enthralling future. As we sail into uncharted territories of prospect and innovation, DAOs promise to play a leading role in the sophisticated dance of technology and economics.

Chapter 7. Rethinking Supply Chains: The Role of Blockchain

Just as the industrial revolutions of the past completely transformed the way our society functions, the emerging Fourth Industrial Revolution, largely driven by digital technologies, holds the potential to dramatically reshape our world once more. Within this context, few technologies hold as much potential as blockchain. In particular, its applications in revolutionizing supply chain management could very well be an early indication of the sweeping changes on the horizon.

7.1. The Essence of a Supply Chain - A Brief Overview

To appreciate the potential of blockchain in reimagining supply chains, it is essential first to understand what these chains are and why they are critical. Supply chains represent the sequence of processes involved in the production and distribution of a commodity. This includes everything from sourcing raw materials to delivering the end product to the consumer.

A key factor in any supply chain is the flow of goods, information, and cash. Each stage of a product's journey should be traceable, and any piece of information - about origin, ownership, location, and more - must be readily available. However, the existing systems aren't fully effective in enabling this traceability and transparency, which is where blockchain comes into the picture.

7.2. Blockchain: An Introduction

In essence, a blockchain is a continuously growing list of records, known as blocks, which are linked and secured using cryptography. Once data is stored in a block, it is extremely difficult to change it. This makes any information stored on a blockchain tamper-proof. Moreover, because every participant in a blockchain network has a full copy of the entire chain, it is also transparent and decentralized, free from the potential interference or control of a single party.

7.3. Blockchain's Transformative Role in Supply Chains

Since blockchain technology provides an immutable record and ensures data transparency, it can contribute significantly to making supply chain processes more secure, reliable, and efficient. This may include:

1. Counterfeit Protection: Counterfeiting is a major issue in several industries. Blockchain technology can help to overcome this problem by making product histories transparent and immutable. Consumers could use a blockchain-based system to verify that a product has been genuinely created by its purported manufacturer.

2. Track and Trace: Real-time tracking of goods as they move through the supply chain can ensure that they have not been tamely stored at some point, potentially avoiding spoilages or deliberate damages. Blockchain could potentially create an unbroken chain of custody log for goods.

3. Auditability: Auditing a supply chain can be time-consuming, especially for products with long and complex chains. Blockchain can make this process faster and more reliable by providing an easily accessible, tamper-proof record of the history of an item.

7.4. Applying Blockchain to Supply Chains - Examples in Practice

To better understand the potential of blockchain for supply chains, it could be useful to look at some examples of its current use. IBM and Maersk, for instance, have jointly developed TradeLens, a blockchain-based shipping solution designed to promote more efficient and secure global trade. This solution enhances transparency and collaboration across the shipping supply chain ecosystem.

On the other hand, De Beers, the diamond giant, launched Tracr, a blockchain platform that enables a digital trail for each diamond, from the mine right down to the consumer. This has gone a long way in curtailing the production and distribution of conflict diamonds.

7.5. Advancing Forward: The Future of Blockchain in Supply Chains

The potential for blockchain-enhanced supply chains is vast. In the near future, we may see blockchain being used to create decentralized marketplaces that offer unprecedented security and convenience to buyers and sellers. It might also help in building more sustainable and ethical supply chains, as businesses become more cognizant of their environmental and social impacts.

Blockchain also blends elegantly with other technologies like IoT and AI to improve predictive capabilities, increase transparency, and facilitate autonomous decisions within supply chains. An operator could use IoT devices and blockchain to monitor goods around the clock, while AI can anticipate potential issues and adjust accordingly.

However, with all these potential benefits, blockchain implementation is not without challenges. Integration with existing infrastructure, scalability, legal and regulatory issues, and user adoption remain significant concerns. This necessitates continued investment in research and development and proactive stakeholder education.

Such a transformative journey will surely invite a fine blend of anticipation and anxiety, but it's crucial to remember that we stand at the threshold of a new era. Blockchain has the potential to bring about a level of transparency and efficiency to supply chains that could, in many respects, democratize access to ethical and sustainable products. This is not just a competitive advantage—it's a massive leap towards a more equitable and sustainable global economy.

Chapter 8. Impacts on Global Trade: Blockchain in International Commerce

The turn of the century has seen the rise of digital technologies, with the eminence of blockchain proving to be significantly disruptive – especially in international trade. The functioning of global commerce, an intricate machine dependent upon trust, intermediation, and efficient management of information, has been ripe for transformation through this technology.

8.1. An Overview

Blockchains, at heart, are decentralized, distributed ledgers recording transactions across multiple computers so that any involved record cannot be altered retroactively, without altering all subsequent blocks. The properties of immutability, transparency, and autonomy that blockchain technology offers, all juxtapose the friction and tediousness systemic in conventional methods of international trade.

Traditionally, global trade is filled with paper trails and slow-moving, bureaucratic systems—legacy infrastructures that are prone to fraud, delays, and human error. Trade finance, cross-border transactions, supply chain management, and trust in trade, stand as prominent obstacles that could be addressed by leveraging blockchain.

8.2. Trade Finance and Cross-Border Transactions

A key application of this technology with potential disruptions in international trade is Trade Finance and cross-border transactions. The global nature and complexity of trade finance operations involve numerous participants, like banks, insurers, Customs and Border Protection (CBP), buyers, and sellers. The paperwork related to these transactions is often manual, paper-based, low in transparency, and subjected to delays and errors.

Blockchain can streamline this process. Blockchain-based smart contracts—digital protocols that automate the execution of a contract—can make transaction processes faster, cheaper, more transparent and secure. Smart contracts trigger themselves on the completion of certain prerequisites, such as the receipt of goods, eliminating intermediaries and facilitating quicker transactions. Consequently, the costs related to auditing, paperwork, and errors could dramatically reduce.

In cross-border transactions, by providing a single, immutable record, blockchain can alleviate the necessity for reconciliation of different ledgers maintained by different participants. Moreover, the decentralized nature of blockchain removes the need for a central bank, thus cutting down on transfer times and eradicating extra costs.

8.3. Supply Chain Management

Another sphere with profound implications is supply chain management. In essence, a supply chain is a network between a company and its suppliers to produce and distribute a specific product, and the blockchain has the power to encourage optimal reliability and transparency.

The lack of transparency and traceability in traditional supply chains can lead to counterfeiting, delays, and inefficiencies. Blockchain can enhance supply chain management through real-time, secure information sharing and documentation of product origin. With every product or component linked to a blockchain that records its journey from origin to customer, it is possible to attain an unprecedented level of transparency.

This way, blockchain could ensure product authenticity, identify issues and irregularities instantly, improve recall management, and unveil unethical practices. Certainly, it will take time and effort to implement blockchain at each stage of the product journey, but the benefits will undoubtedly exceed the costs in the longer run.

8.4. Trust in Trade

Trust in international trade has always been of paramount importance and is facilitated by intermediaries such as banks and regulatory authorities. These intermediaries not only increase the overall cost of global trade but also introduce inefficiencies and delays.

Blockchain, built on foundations of transparency and immutability, offers an alternative. It can instill trust within the participants by creating an indelible history of transactions that can be verified by all parties involved. A universal ledger of transactions, like the one blockchain offers, reduces fraud and reinforces trust—a cornerstone in international trade.

8.5. Looking Ahead

While blockchain's potential to transform international commerce appears promising, a successful implementation requires sustained collaboration amongst all stakeholders. Several groundbreaking experiments and pilot projects by organizations and consortia are already hinting at a future where the traditional means of international trade are overhauled. But significant challenges, including interoperability, regulatory environment, and the digital divide, must be overcome.

Despite these challenges, blockchain's impact on international commerce marks an inflection point in economic history, offering the promise to redefine international trade's antiquated systems. As we move forward into the latter part of this century, blockchain stands poised to transform the world of commerce — international and otherwise — with its disruptive potential. The path may be arduous, but the potential reward could radically alter the global economy's landscape. A proactive approach in understanding and deploying this technology could position stakeholders advantageously in this digital revolution – a revolution that will undoubtedly redefine the contours of global trade.

Chapter 9. Surviving Cyber Threats: Blockchain in Ensuring Security & Privacy

In an increasingly digital world, the protection against cyber threats ranks among the topmost concerns. As both business and personal life migrate to a virtual environment, ensuring security and privacy of information has become a mammoth task. Here, the role of blockchain technology enters, casting light on new and efficient strategies to combat these threats. Undoubtedly, the paradigm shift to blockchain technology may emerge as a robust answer to these lingering cybersecurity threats.

9.1. The Blockchain: An Overview

At a fundamental level, blockchain is, as the name indicates, a chain of blocks. However, instead of traditional physical blocks, these are digital pieces of information (the "blocks") stored in a public database (the "chain"). The blocks contain information about transactions, say, date, time, and dollar amount of your most recent purchase from Amazon. Blocks store information that distinct them from other blocks, much like you and your name distinguish you from other humans. The unique codes called "hash" secure the individual blocks.

Blockchain's architecture inherently resists data modification, a principle that heightens its appeal in the context of cybersecurity. Once a block enters the chain, changing or tampering with the information becomes exceptionally challenging, ensuring data integrity and a level of immutability.

9.2. Amidst the Cyber Threat Landscape

In the increasingly networked world, cybersecurity threats loom large. Cybercriminals leverage the interconnected digital milieu to exploit individuals, businesses, and even governments. From data breaches, password cracking, ransomware to phishing attacks, the list of potential cyber risks expands with every passing day. In such a scenario, blockchain's potential in bolstering security and privacy becomes a compelling narrative.

Blockchains decentralize data, contrasting with traditional systems where data exists on a central server ripe for hacking. By distributing data across numerous nodes, blockchain reduces the possibility of successful cyber-attacks.

9.3. Guarding Privacy through Pseudonymity

Blockchain systems usually offer pseudonymous transactions, displaying codes instead of actual user identities. Although transactions can be traced back, it is challenging to connect them directly to users. This pseudonymity can help ensure user privacy on the internet, a safe ground against identity theft and unwanted tracking.

While this doesn't provide complete anonymity, it certainly provides a degree of privacy. Users control their data and decide what, how, and when to share their information. They can engage in transactions without divulging excessive personal details.

9.4. Fortifying Authentication and Verification Procedures

Blockchain solutions can revolutionize traditional authentication processes. By leveraging the technology's immutable and decentralized nature, the process of identity verification can become more reliable, simple, and secure.

A blockchain-based ID verification mechanism can significantly reduce the likelihood of identity theft, data breaches, and unauthorized access. Every request for access can be logged, verified, and approved in a transparent manner, thereby reinforcing the system's security.

9.5. Enhancing Data Integrity

Data integrity relates to maintaining and assuring the accuracy and consistency of data over its entire lifecycle. Today, in a world teeming with sophisticated cyber threats, ensuring data integrity is crucial and complex.

Blockchain technology, with its immutable and transparent nature, can enrich data integrity. Once a transaction is recorded on a blockchain, it becomes almost impossible to alter or delete. Any alteration attempt necessitates a consensus from the blockchain network, which is extremely challenging to achieve. Thus, blockchain can stand as the sentinel, guarding data and maintaining its integrity.

9.6. Countering DDoS Attacks

Distributed Denial of Service (DDoS) attacks flood a network with superfluous requests, thereby making the system unavailable to its intended users. However, a blockchain-based DNS could distribute the contents to a larger number of nodes, making DDoS attacks ineffective.

In blockchain-based DNS systems, the domain information is distributed across multiple nodes, which can effectively combat the vulnerability arising from a central point of failure, as seen in traditional web hosting.

9.7. Conclusion: A Step Towards Secure Future

Blockchain technology, with its impressive capabilities, provides a holistic approach to cybersecurity without compromising data privacy, integrity, and accessibility. Although its full potential is yet to be explored, it is increasingly becoming a seminal force in framing a robust cybersecurity landscape. By embedding blockchain's decentralized and transparent paradigm into cybersecurity tactics, we can envisage a future secured against the alarming spate of cyber threats.

In the forthcoming chapters, we will delve further into blockchain's other potential impacts on the global economy, digital identity, smart contracts, governance, and more, hoping to instigate even the most hesitant among us to consider its potential seriously.

Chapter 10. Regulation and Policy: National and International Perspectives

The mantle of regulation is a multifaceted one, being both an enabler and a controller. In the realm of blockchain and cryptocurrency, these regulatory constructs have an essential role in shaping the landscape.

10.1. National Perspectives: Towards Comprehensive Regulations

The regulatory approaches towards blockchain at a national level are a complex tapestry woven with individual threads of innovation, protection, and legality. Let's begin our exploration in different corners of the world.

10.1.1. United States: A Juggling Act

The U.S, known for its vibrant tech scene, faces a conundrum. On one hand, it needs to promote blockchain innovation for economic growth, and on the other, it must ensure stability and security in the markets. The Securities and Exchange Commission (SEC) and the Commodity Futures Trading Commission (CFTC) are two primary regulators, seeking to prevent fraud and manipulation. The Internal Revenue Service (IRS) classifies cryptocurrencies as property for taxation. These regulatory bodies are still evolving their approaches to accommodate the unique aspects of blockchain, allowing room for substantial evolution in the coming years.

10.1.2. China: Perceptive Pragmatism

China offers an interesting dichotomy. The Chinese government has maintained a hard stance against cryptocurrencies, considering them a threat to financial stability. Simultaneously, it has recognized and promoted the potential of blockchain technology. Embracing regulation by endorsing "RegTech," it advances regulatory goals through technological innovation– enabling efficient market supervision and nurturing blockchain potentialities.

10.1.3. European Union: An Embodiment of Adaptive Legislation

Europe has adopted a more inclusive vision towards blockchain and cryptocurrencies. However, the states within the EU have varying stances. While countries like Malta and Estonia are known for their pro-blockchain laws, others have not been as quick to adopt favorable legislation. The EU is striving to develop a comprehensive framework for blockchain regulation, harnessing the technology's potential while mitigating risks associated with it.

10.2. Cryptocurrency Regulations: A Global Arena

One cannot talk about blockchain without discussing the elephant in the room—cryptocurrencies. Here's how different jurisdictions have approached the regulation of this unique product of blockchain.

10.2.1. United States: Straddling Two Worlds

In the American regulatory environment, cryptocurrencies straddle the line between currencies and securities, a distinction that drives the regulatory approach. Many cryptocurrencies are categorized as securities, placing them under the SEC's purview. Those that function as currencies are subjected to a different set of regulations, governed primarily by the U.S. Treasury's Financial Crimes Enforcement Network (FinCEN).

10.2.2. South Korea: From Resistance to Acceptance

Initially apprehensive, South Korea has evolved towards acceptance of cryptocurrencies, brought about by methodical regulation. In March 2020, South Korea's National Assembly passed laws that provide a comprehensive legal framework for cryptocurrencies and exchanges.

10.2.3. Japan: Endorsing the New Economy

Japan has conspicuously embraced cryptocurrencies, affording them legal status as a payment method. Japan's Financial Services Agency (FSA) exercises rigorous entity-level regulations for cryptocurrency exchanges to mitigate malpractices and protect consumers.

10.3. International Perspectives: Keeping Up with the Pace

In the international arena, organizations like the Financial Stability Board (FSB), the International Monetary Fund (IMF), and the Bank for International Settlements (BIS) play a crucial role in sculpting the global response.

10.4. The United Nations: An Agent of Change

The United Nations has recognized the consequences of blockchain technology on the financial systems and has worked towards wielding its potential to achieve Sustainable Development Goals (SDGs). The UN Innovation Network, an informal association of UN agencies, focuses on research and applications of blockchain towards humanitarian causes.

10.5. The International Monetary Fund (IMF) and the World Bank: Breaching Borders with Digital Currency

The IMF and the World Bank, understanding the international implications of cryptocurrencies, have fostered a proactive stance. They've closely worked on "Learning Coin," a blockchain-based cryptocurrency project, to investigate the challenges, benefits, and technological aspects tied to digital currencies and distributed ledger technologies.

10.6. The Conclusion: Taming the Wild West

Regulation in the blockchain era is no less than taming a wild horse. While the potential for disruption is high, this disruption needs to be directed to produce constructive change. Legislation needs to keep pace with this high-stakes race and indeed, regulators around the world are contributing to this colossal endeavour by gradually moving towards a regulatory consensus. As we move forward, it's clear that one size does not fit all. With unique challenges in each country, the potentialities of blockchain demand flexible, adaptive, and well-thought-out regulatory policies.

Chapter 11. Futuristic Outlook: The Potential Economic Influence of a Blockchain-Dominant World

To understand the economic influence of a blockchain-dominant world, it's crucial to contextualize its birth, scope, and potential. When Satoshi Nakamoto first unveiled the Bitcoin protocol in the late 2000s, it was lauded for its revolutionary approach to decentralized financial transactions. However, less than a decade later, the implications of Nakamoto's technology – blockchain – have far surpassed the world of cryptocurrency. Today, blockchain's potential extends across every facet of our lives, from revolutionizing global trade to transforming democratic governance.

11.1. Shedding the Shackles of Centralized Systems

Blockchain is essentially a decentralized, trustless, and immutable data management system. Constantly updated, yet infinitely secure, it surpasses the limitations of traditional, centralized systems. By eliminating intermediaries and gatekeepers, blockchain reduces friction in transactions, leading to increased efficiency and reduced costs.

Central banks, bureaucratic red tape, and multinational corporations have long dictated the world's financial systems. However, a blockchain-dominant world could dilute these power structures. Economic control would shift to individual hands, fostering a truly democratized financial world.

From sending remittances across borders to tokenization of physical assets, the possibilities are almost limitless. In agriculture, for example, blockchain can track and verify the entire supply chain, providing transparency and authenticity to consumers. It can also aid farmers in proving rightful ownership of their lands, expediting access to essential resources such as credit.

In healthcare, blockchain can create an indisputable, time-stamped record of patient data that can be securely shared amongst clinicians, improving service quality and patient satisfaction. Furthermore, it can enhance research collaborations by providing a secure data-sharing platform, propelling us into a new era of scientific discovery.

11.2. Understanding Smart Contracts: An Economic Game-Changer

One of the most transformative technological applications within the blockchain realm is the implementation of smart contracts. These are self-executing contracts with the terms of agreement directly written into code. They exist across a distributed, decentralized blockchain network which ensures that they are transparent, traceable, and irreversible.

Smart contracts automatically execute when agreed conditions are met, reducing the need for intermediaries, increasing transaction speed, and decreasing costs. This removes a multitude of hurdles for businesses, including contract costs, navigating legalese, and enforcing contractual obligations.

In industries like real estate, this can revolutionize the way we buy, sell, and rent properties. By implementing smart contracts, property transactions can occur directly between buyer and seller, eliminating the need for real estate agents, mortgage brokers, or deed companies.

Not only can this lead to considerable cost savings, but it also minimizes the risks associated with fraud.

11.3. Tokenization — The Gateway to Liquidity and Interoperability

Tokenization refers to the process of converting real-world assets—say a piece of art, a house, or a share of a company—into digital tokens that can be stored, transferred, and exchanged on a blockchain. This can unlock the untapped value of illiquid assets by enabling fractional ownership, increasing market participation, providing access to global investors, and offering unprecedented liquidity.

A painting worth millions, for instance, could be tokenized into smaller, affordable units, permitting a larger group of investors to own a slice. The implications of this democratization of asset ownership would be groundbreaking, enabling economic participation on a global scale irrespective of capital constraints.

Furthermore, blockchain's inherent interoperability could allow the seamless exchange of these tokens across diverse markets. This would create a truly global, unified, and frictionless economy.

11.4. Revamping Global Trade and The Supply Chain

Blockchain's potential far surpasses individual sectors, promising to revolutionize the way we conduct global trade. It can create a transparent, secure, and efficient platform where records of trades can be kept, validated, and shared.

Each product can be traced from its source, ensuring health and safety standards, rooting out counterfeit goods, and upholding brand integrity. In a world fraught with uncertainty and deceit, this transparency is invaluable.

High-value industries such as pharmaceuticals, luxury goods, and electronics could particularly benefit from adopting this technology to counteract issues with counterfeit goods which annually cost these industries billions. Consumers, too, would greatly benefit from knowing the authenticity of their purchases.

Moreover, the logistics sector could utilize blockchain to streamline complex procedures, reducing paperwork, and ensuring timely product delivery.

Implementation of blockchain technology in global trade can lead to a reduction in systemic inefficiencies and a substantial boost to global GDP.

11.5. The Challenges and Potential Setbacks

While the advent of a blockchain-dominant world unlocks many opportunities, it is not devoid of challenges. Issues pertaining to scalability, data privacy, regulatory oversight, and technology adoption rate are significant obstacles that must be addressed.

Moreover, the predominant "proof of work" algorithm that secures most blockchains is resource-intensive and has raised environmental concerns. While solutions such as proof of stake are being explored, they are yet to be fully implemented and tested at scale.

A world where wealth and power are continually decentralized would not be without its struggles. Governments, businesses, and individuals must adapt and be prepared to tackle issues relating to data privacy, cybersecurity, and regulation.

11.6. Conclusion: A Quantum Leap Towards an Equitable Future?

A blockchain-dominant world symbolizes far more than a techno-economic evolution; it signifies a societal paradigm shift towards decentralization, transparency, and equality. It presents an opportunity for a seismic economic transformation that moves power from institutions to individuals.

However, just as with any emerging technology, blockchain comes with its limitations and concerns that need to be thoughtfully addressed. It's imperative that as we move towards harnessing this technology, we remain cognizant of its potential impacts, retaining our human-centric approach in a rapidly evolving digital world.

Ultimately, it is not blockchain, but how we utilize it, that will determine whether it becomes a key driver of economic innovation or just another fleeting technological phenomenon. It beckons us to approach this threshold with optimism, insight, and a willingness to shape this new world for our collective benefit.

www.ingramcontent.com/pod-product-compliance
Lightning Source LLC
Chambersburg PA
CBHW062303290526
45794CB00006B/2673